America's Forgotten Slaves: The History of Native American Slavery in the New World and the United States

By Charles River Editors

A 16th century depiction of natives being enslaved by the Spanish

About Charles River Editors

Charles River Editors is a boutique digital publishing company, specializing in bringing history back to life with educational and engaging books on a wide range of topics. Keep up to date with our new and free offerings with this 5 second sign up on our weekly mailing list, and visit Our Kindle Author Page to see other recently published Kindle titles.

We make these books for you and always want to know our readers' opinions, so we encourage you to leave reviews and look forward to publishing new and exciting titles each week.

Introduction

"The carrying of Negroes among the Indians has all along been thought detrimental, as an intimacy ought to be avoided." – A passage from a 1751 South Carolina law

It has often been said that the greatest invention of all time was the sail, which facilitated the internationalization of the globe and thus ushered in the modern era. Columbus' contact with the New World, alongside European maritime contact with the Far East, transformed human history, and in particular the history of Africa.

It was the sail that linked the continents of Africa and America, and thus it was also the sail that facilitated the greatest involuntary human migration of all time. The African slave trade is a complex and deeply divisive subject that has had a tendency to evolve according the political requirements of any given age, and is often touchable only with the correct distribution of culpability. It has for many years, therefore, been deemed singularly unpalatable to implicate Africans themselves in the perpetration of the institution, and only in recent years has the large-scale African involvement in both the Atlantic and Indian Ocean Slave Trades come to be an accepted fact. There can, however, be no doubt that even though large numbers of indigenous Africans were liable, it was European ingenuity and greed that fundamentally drove the industrialization of the Transatlantic slave trade in response to massive new market demands created by their equally ruthless exploitation of the Americas.

In time, the Atlantic slave trade provided for the labor requirements of the emerging plantation economies of the New World. It was a specific, dedicated and industrial enterprise wherein huge profits were at stake, and a vast and highly organized network of procurement, processing, transport and sale existed to expedite what was in effect a modern commodity market. It existed without sentimentality, without history, and without tradition, and it was only outlawed once the advances of the industrial revolution had created alternative sources of energy for agricultural production.

The African slave trade is a complex and deeply divisive subject that has had a tendency to evolve according the political requirements of any given era, and it is often touchable only with the correct distribution of culpability. There can be no doubt that even though large numbers of others were liable, it was European ingenuity and greed that fundamentally drove the industrialization of the Transatlantic slave trade in response to massive new market demands created by their equally ruthless exploitation of the Americas.

Most Americans are familiar with the extent and costs of slavery as a result of that slave trade, and people generally know that slavery existed around the world. The Krim Tatar allies of the Ottomans conducted almost annual slave raids into Ukraine, Russia and Poland for 200 years, and the trade between sub-Saharan Africa and the Muslim north involved salt, gold and lots of slaves. Muslim corsairs from the Barbary coasts raided across the Mediterranean for centuries, with Christian raiders returning the favor. The East African slave trade was also large, and lasted centuries. That said, while the Transatlantic slave trade didn't last as long as those others, it was the largest of them all, with an estimated 11 million slaves shipped from Africa to the Americas.

What far less people are familiar with are the other forms of slavery in America, and the victims who were enslaved. Sizable numbers of Native Americans were enslaved, with some of them working alongside African slaves in the fields and others shipped off to the sugar islands. The total number of natives enslaved over the whole colonial period for both American continents is estimated at somewhere between 2.4 and 4.9 million, while estimates for North America north of Mexico are 141,000 to 340,000. These estimates do not seem to include slaves held by the native peoples themselves, nor do they include the serf-like status still a bit short of slavery that was imposed on millions of others.

Prior to the European colonization of what is now the United States, native groups themselves took captives. Men were often killed, and children were incorporated into their captors' tribe, but there were hundreds of tribal peoples and many variants on the fate of captives. In the Pacific Northwest, slaves were killed in rituals, including being ritually cannibalized. After the arrival of the Europeans, the number of captives increased, and their fates became intertwined with the colonists and their African slaves.

In the Southwest, there was a slave trade in New Mexico and northern Mexico involving captives for use as domestic servants and sales to the silver mines in Mexico. The formidable Comanches were just another nomadic group until they were exposed to horses (probably from stock released during the Pueblo rebellion of 1680 in New Mexico). They formed a new culture and became an almost imperial force, which involved conducting raids for slaves.

Afro-Tejano slaves in Spanish Texas had different social circumstances than slaves held in the later Texas Republic. In the Southeast, slave raiding and trading involved the colonies of the English, Spanish and French. Moreover, several thousand free African Americans owned slaves and slavery in the United States did not end with freeing slaves in the South in 1865.

There were even some American white slaves with African masters. After independence was achieved, the American colonies no longer had the protection of the Royal Navy, and that made American shipping prey for the North African corsairs based in Algiers, Tunis and Tripoli, known as the Barbary Pirates. They captured a good many American merchant ships and enslaved the crews. Some were ransomed and some vanished into North African society.

The Barbary Pirates' main source of income was extortion. The United States paid a large amount of money to obtain the release of enslaved sailors and to obtain immunity from attack. Public outrage over the payment of tribute to Muslim pirates led to the creation of the Navy Department and the construction of some powerful frigates. America went on to fight two wars against the Barbary Pirates in 1801-1805 and in 1815, marking the country's first conflicts over slavery.

America's Forgotten Slaves: The History of Native American Slavery in the New World and the United States examines the different systems of slavery practiced across America. Along with pictures depicting important people, places, and events, you will learn about America's forgotten slaves like never before.

America's Forgotten Slaves: The History of Native American Slavery in the New World and the United States

About Charles River Editors

Introduction

    The Indian Slave Trade in the Southeast

    The Transportation of Criminals

    Indian Slavery in the Northeast and New France

    Indian Slavery in the Pacific Northwest

    Slavery in the Southwest and California

    Indian Owners of African Slaves

    Black Slaveowners

    The End of Slavery

    Online Resources

    Further Reading

Free Books by Charles River Editors

Discounted Books by Charles River Editors

The Indian Slave Trade in the Southeast

Slavery among the various Indian peoples in what is now the United States took a wide variety of forms. Often, slavery was less a matter of captive labor than it was a matter of status, as slaves enhanced the social status of the owner and also served as a kind of evidence of victory over an enemy. Essentially, Indian slaves created social capital. Indian slavery varied a great deal, but generally they gave the slaves more actual rights than the predominant chattel slavery of African Americans, and slavery was not always a permanent, inheritable condition. European slavery was generally for life as slave status was inheritable. Slavery focused on producing wealth by producing valuable commodity cops like tobacco, indigo, rice and cotton and wealth supplied the status (Gallay 8).

The first Indian captives known to reach Europe were taken captive by the Vikings during their brief settlement in Newfoundland. The Vikings captured two Beothuk boys, but the boys do not appear to have been considered slaves or servants. They were taken to Norway in 1009, baptized, and taught Norse (Weaver 36).

Europeans taking Indians captive was common. Columbus' 1493 voyage to America was a relatively gargantuan expedition, consisting of 17 ships and 1,500 colonists, and for the return voyage to Spain, some 1,500 natives were rounded up and 500 selected to take on the return. Of these, nearly 200 died on the voyage, while the rest were sold in Seville as slaves and most quickly died (Weaver 48). Despite early royal condemnation of taking Indians as slaves, several thousand Indians were sold in Spain and became servants.

The explorer Gaspar Corte Real was commissioned in 1500 by the Portuguese king to find the Northwest Passage. The fabled passage wasn't found, but two of his ships returned to Portugal with 55 Beothuk captives aboard, and they were sold as slaves to defray some of the voyage's costs (Weaver 56).

Some of what is known about Indian slavery in Europe stems from court cases in Spain where several thousand Indians worked as slaves, mostly in domestic service. Since the Spanish had outlawed enslaving Indians, some Indians in Spain were able to successfully sue for their freedom.

Slavery in Spanish America was made even more complicated by the presence of Asian slaves. The Manila Galleons ran from Acapulco to Manila in Spanish Asia for 250 years, and some of the cargo they brought back to Mexico were slaves who were known to be Filipino, Chinese, even Japanese and people from India.

In what is now the American Southeast, the pre-European Indian population was substantial. The people were primarily settled in villages, sustaining themselves on the "Three Sisters" (corn, squash, and beans) and hunting. There were still some remnants of the older Mississippian culture, notably the Natchez.

The Spanish under Ponce de Leon explored Florida in 1513, and then came the momentously large expedition led by Hernando de Soto. The de Soto expedition tramped over much of the Southeast in the years 1539-42, and it unleashed a whirlwind of violence and disease that took countless lives and resulted in the deaths of most members of the expedition. It completely disrupted the old relationships among the tribes, and diseases introduced by the de Soto expedition depopulated much of the region.

An engraving of de Soto

During de Soto's march, the Spanish commandeered Indian crops and bodies, using the captives to carry supplies and treating them as expendable slaves. The Spaniards took what they needed, often destroying what they did not take. Indian resistance was fierce, however, and they killed many of the Spanish. The tough Spanish endured privations and discomfort, but most of them died in the futile search for another rich kingdom like those of the Inca and Aztec.

There were a few attempts at Spanish settlement on the Southeastern mainland, notably in Florida, where St. Augustine dates to 1565 and recent archaeology indicates that Pensacola may date to 1559. The Spanish early on depopulated the Antilles and Bahamas in search for Indians to enslave for labor in Hispaniola, but when Mexico was colonized, Spanish efforts shifted there from the islands, leaving them as a kind of colonial backwater.

Still, gradually the Spanish set up a chain of missions designed to convert the Indians and gather them into settlements. They were moderately successful, with a chain of missions stretching along the Florida Panhandle and up along the Georgia coast. Things changed in the 1600s when the English established the Virginia colony, followed by the Carolinas and eventually, Georgia.

The economy of the colonists in South Carolina in the colony's first few decades depended heavily on trading with the Indians. Three items stood out in the trade: furs, deer hides, and slaves. There were some changes that fed back into each other and led to the disruption of Indian populations for hundreds of miles inland. For example, guns made it easier to hunt and kill deer, and the furs and deer hides - and captives - bought guns, ammunition, tools, horses and many other things that led to dependency on the trade and dependency on the Carolinian traders. Processing the furs and hides was hard work. Traditionally, it was women's work, but as the trade in hides grew, the workload grew, and with it the need for more labor. Raiding for captives to sell as slaves also produced captive women who provided the labor to process the hides.

In time, more pressure on the deer population reduced their numbers and led to an increase in conflicts between the tribes over the deer. The better-armed tribes took over the resources, and in the process took captives. All these things reinforced each other, and eventually guns cost 12-16 deer hides, depending on the quality of the hides. A single slave could buy a gun, ammunition, a horse, a hatchet, and clothes (Taylor 231).

The Carolinians pushed the gun trade with the tribes, and arming Indians might at first seem foolhardy since it gave them the means to attack the colonists, but providing some tribes with guns built a tribal dependency on the Carolinians for more guns, gunpowder, and shot, which the Indians could not make for themselves. Thus, some tribes began to raid for slaves to trade for guns and supplies, and from the Carolinians' viewpoint, this had a double benefit of weakening potential tribal opposition and building a dependency relationship of allied tribes (Taylor 228).

Because of the danger of escape, most Indian captives were not enslaved in the Carolinas, but were sold in the Caribbean, especially in Barbados. Indian captives were sometimes traded for African slaves on a two-for-one basis, with two Indians being the equivalent of one African. As with most forms of slavery, participants gave several justifications to rationalize enslaving people. Among the justifications were that Indian captives faced torture and death at the hands of other Indians, so slavery was a better condition. The opportunity for Indian captives to become Christian and thereby save their souls was also used as a justification (Taylor 231).

Inevitably, the Southeastern slave trade was enormously destructive, not just of tribes in the Carolinas, but also in Georgia and Florida (Florida was then Spanish territory). The war with the Stono Indians in 1674 and the Westo War in 1680 were partly caused by the depredations of the slave trade (Brown 119). The pre-colonial relationship among the Southeastern tribes was profoundly affected, and over time, a number of tribes were destroyed.

Before the slave trade and the raids, the Spanish mission system in Florida was rather successful, with about 25,000 Indians settled in Christian-oriented village communities managed by priests, much like the better-known missions in California. These missions were not just in Florida - they ranged well into Georgia. Slave raiding by Indians allied with the Carolinians and catastrophic damage caused by English colonists who led other Indian allies eventually destroyed the system, to the point that by 1706, the original 25,000 mission Indians were reduced to just 400 (Worth 296).

The raids for slaves merged with colonial participation in a European war, the War of the Spanish Succession. Fought from 1701-1714, it was called Queen Anne's War in the English colonies, and the most destructive period for the Florida missions was between 1704 and 1706, when raiders from Georgia and the Carolinas, often Indians in association with colonists, devastated Florida. In a sense, Queen Anne's War was a pretext for the most intense slave raiding in American history. They destroyed 32 villages, killed priests, burned the churches, and ultimately enslaved about 10,000 people. (Taylor 233).

The slave trade was a catastrophe for Spanish Florida. Through 1715, at least 15,000-20,000 Florida Indians were enslaved, and that is probably a low-end estimate (Gallay 295). The Spanish missions were destroyed, and most of the already thinly populated areas were depopulated as slave raiders made raids all the way to the Florida Keys.

The slave trade was also a major blow to other tribes. Perhaps 1,500 Choctaw had been enslaved, and perhaps 1,200 Tuscarora (Gallay 298). After that, the Tuscarora were broken and the remnants fled north, but the Choctaw emerged unified and fairly powerful.

Perhaps the worst nightmare for Carolinians in that era was the potential of an alliance between the tribes and African slaves. White slaveholders deliberately emphasized Indian cruelty to their slaves, trying to drive a wedge between African slaves and the Indians. Had African slaves managed to join the tribes and conduct a joint rebellion, they could probably have wiped out the Carolinians (McLaughlin 369-70).

The war that shook South Carolina saw something like that very nearly happen. The Yamasees had been slave raiders, but they rebelled in 1715 and began liberating African slaves, some of whom fought with them. The Carolinians actually armed African slaves to fight the Yamasee, an indication of the conflict's desperation (Gallay 347-48). The Yamasee were defeated, but it was an uncomfortably close call.

In March 1713, a South Carolina force, operating at the request of North Carolina, intervened in North Carolina's fight against the Tuscaroras. Commanded by Captain James Moore, Jr., the force consisted primarily of allied Indians (including Yamasee, Cherokee, and Creek), and they stormed and burned the main Tuscarora village, killing hundreds. They executed 166 men, then took 392 women and children back to Charleston for sale. The Tuscarora survivors fled north to the Iroquois, eventually becoming the Iroquois' sixth nation (Taylor 234).

Indian slavery was quite important in the early colonial period, but its importance faded in the mid-18th century. The Yamasee War of 1715 demonstrated that Indians were potentially dangerous slaves. The Yamasee were a warlike tribe that had cooperated with the Carolinians, but they had not provided enough captives to pay their debts to traders. The traders threatened to enslave members of the tribe because debts were not being paid, and the Yamasee took the threat seriously enough to instigate a war (Worth 302).

After the Yamasee War, Indian slavery in the region mostly faded away, if only because there were far fewer potential slaves. Tribes in the deep interior remained numerous, but the threat to the heartland of the South Carolina colony was removed. The Indian trade shrank but remained, and Indians were employed to track down escaped African slaves, although sometimes the Indians tried to sell recaptured slaves in Florida or Louisiana.

A quirk in the laws about slavery was that slave status followed that of the mother. If the father was white or Indian and the mother a slave, the children were slaves, but if the father was a slave and the mother free, the children were free. That meant that slaves with Indian ancestry through a woman had an argument that they should be free. Slave law gave slaves few rights, but they were permitted to allege illegal enslavement.

In 1772, a future Founding Father, George Mason, represented a slave named Robin and 11 others. They alleged that maternal descent should have made them free. Mason argued the case in the General Court in Virginia, and the Court agreed, setting them free. Later, in 1806, the courts declared that enslaved descendants of Indians were free (Ablavsky 1457, 1460).

Mason

All this time, Spain controlled Florida, and after the French were defeated in Canada by the British in the French & Indian War, the French territory in Louisiana and the Mississippi Valley was turned over to Spain, which held it until the 1803 Louisiana Purchase. In Spanish law, Indians were theoretically free vassals of the Crown and could not be enslaved, but Indian slavery persisted in Louisiana. For example, a 1776 census showed 1,540 African slaves and 229 Indian slaves. During the 1790s, several Indian slaves sued for their freedom on the grounds that by Spanish law they should be free. The results of those suits are not known (Webre 125-26).

Black slaves had some rights under Spanish law, and slaves were allowed to own property and to appear in court as a party in a lawsuit. In what would be incomprehensible to American slaveholders, slaves in Louisiana could sue their masters (Webre 122). Over the Spanish period, the number of slaves in Louisiana increased from 5,000-20,000, but very few were Indian.

The Transportation of Criminals

While the British Empire was spreading and settling colonies in North America, the British had a savage legal code. More than 100 crimes were punishable by death, but a practice had grown up called "Benefit of Clergy" that mercifully tempered the harshness. Descended from medieval times when there were separate court systems for members of the church and for the general population, convicted prisoners, if they could read a passage, were considered to be clergy and were released after being branded on the thumb.

This legal fiction didn't fare well with reforming tendencies of the time, and a new form of tempering harsh justice with a degree of mercy emerged: transportation. Criminals sentenced to transportation were exiled to the colonies, but with the twist that they were sold as indentured servants. The usual term of indenture was seven years, with indenture for capital crimes set at 14 years. It is unclear how many of the convicts transported were for capital crimes, but it seems likely that most such convictions would have resulted in the convict being hanged. All the while, the use of British gallows stayed steady even despite the qualified mercy of transportation.

While this transportation system is more notorious in the British Empire's efforts to colonize Australia and New Zealand, the transportation of convicted felons to the colonies seems to have begun as early as the 1610s, but not much is known about the practice in the early years. Transportation began on a large scale with the passage of the Transportation Act of 1717, which regulated the practice.

The Treasury was contracted with commercial agents to ship convicts to the colonies for a set fee per head. At the start, this was three pounds per each, and it later increased to five pounds. Converting money from that long ago is difficult, but five pounds in 1718 would probably be worth well over $1,000 today, meaning 50,000 convicts at that rate would be worth $50 million.

Given the staggering sums, it must have been one of the larger factors in the trade between the motherland and the colonies. The convict ship would arrive at its destination and colonists could bid for those destined to be indentured servants. It's safe to assume that much like the slave ships, the contractors tried to ensure maximum profits by overloading the ships, providing food and quarters as cheap as necessary only to keep prisoners alive, and then try to make them look as presentable as possible before the auction.

Transportation may have been rationalized as a form of mercy, but it had two other practical advantages, at least to those who were doing the transporting. It physically removed the undesirables from Great Britain, and it provided labor for the colonies. Transported prisoners were released at the end of their term and could legally return home, but premature return was punishable by death.

Not much is known about the total group. The research of records in several British areas regarding transported convicts has shown that about 80% of the convicts were male and 20% female, primarily between the ages of 15 and 29, and guilty of small crimes like petty larceny (Morgan 416). Most of the convicts were unloaded in the mainland colonies between 1718 and 1775, when the prospect of war stopped the process. The total number of convicts transported is unknown, but the generally accepted estimate is 50,000 (although some historians have suggested higher totals, up to 150,000). The 50,000 figure was about a quarter of the British immigrants to go to the mainland American colonies in the 18th century, and it is obviously large total for a colonial British population that reached about 2.5 million (including 500,000 slaves) at the time of the Revolution.

Indentured servants were not technically slaves, and a large number of indentures were voluntary. A typical pattern was a young man who wished to immigrate signed an agreement with an agent, or perhaps a ship captain. The immigrant would get passage to America and the sale of the indenture paid for the passage. Voluntary indentures had rights, and in the colonies themselves, parents sometimes signed indentures for their children who would then become apprentices to learn a trade. Such indentures sometimes specified education, good treatment, and even occasionally tools, clothing, and other items at the end of the indenture. Perhaps the most famous example is young Benjamin Franklin.

Naturally, criminals sentenced to transportation were not seen in a positive light. British society was characterized by a huge gap between the prosperous and the poor. Malnutrition was common, and petty theft was one way that poor people coped. In theory, the theft of a handkerchief could lead to a man being hanged.

As this all suggests, the British elite and political classes were deeply suspicious of the poor. Social conditions were such that poverty was widespread, and British opinion of the convicts sentenced to transportation was that they were scum and worthy of hard labor in stone quarries, or maybe manning the galleys stationed at Gibraltar (Morgan 420-21).

The colonists' opinions of the convicts were equally harsh. People in the colonies strongly resented their colonies being a dumping ground for convicts. A Virginia law in 1748 lumped the convicts with Indians, free blacks, and slaves. Convicts could not serve as witnesses in court, and they could not offer testimony in criminal or civil trials. More than a few Southerners were fearful that the convicts would join with slaves to rebel, and there are instances of convicts and slaves escaping together.

There was also a real concern that the convicts brought disease: British prisons were notoriously foul and full of disease, and the ships bringing them across the Atlantic were probably not much better. What was known as "jail fever" (usually typhus) was not rare in Britain (Morgan 426-27).

An indication of how indentured convicts were regarded is that newspaper notices describing escaped servants were identical to those for escaped slaves. The convicts had certain advantages when they escaped though, most notably their skin color. White skin helped them more readily vanish into the crowd, and many were literate and thus could forge the passes required of traveling slaves and servants.

If they were caught, however, punishment was severe. It was not as severe as the punishment meted out to escaped slaves, but in addition to whatever physical punishment might be given, a month was added to their indentures for each week they were on the loose. A year was added for every month they were gone (Morgan 265-66).

France also tried transporting criminals and undesirables, but this was for a far different reason: the unwillingness of the French to go to Louisiana. The French had trouble attracting settlers to the far more salubrious Canada, and this posed a serious problem for the colony, while the organization in charge of Louisiana, the Company of the West, wanted settlers. Louisiana had a reputation as being a tough place, so almost no one wanted to go there either.

In 1719, the royal authorities opened up a range of institutions that housed orphans, vagrants, and others to the Company to find potential settlers. Several thousand people became available, but obtaining authorization to ship them across the Atlantic was a problem. Among those sent in 1719 were a pickpocket, a man who threatened to kill his mother, and a man arrested multiple times for sodomy (Hardy 211).

In 1720, the Company was authorized to send press gangs into the countryside to arrest and detain for transportation vagabonds, idlers, the unemployed, and jailbirds. These conscription agents were hated and provoked riots, to the extent that 20 of them were murdered in Paris alone.

The majority of the people caught up in the transportation scheme do not seem to have been actual convicts. In 1720, some 600 young people were taken for transit from Paris to a port, with the boys walking chained together and the girls in carts. The resemblance to a slave coffle would have been obvious, and they were exploited ruthlessly by guards and people they met along their way (Hardy 212).

Despite strenuous efforts, the number of convicts and other people transported to Louisiana was small, perhaps less than 900. Most of them ultimately escaped or died. (Hardy 220).

Indian Slavery in the Northeast and New France

When Europeans arrived, most aspects of the tribal peoples were fluid, from food to other resources, so their physical locations often changed and groups might switch loyalty to a new leader. The remnants of tribes shattered by epidemics or war might recombine with each other or move on to exploit new resources.

An example of responding to new environmental opportunities is the Illinois tribe, an Algonquian people who moved out of the lower Great Lakes country into Illinois as the buffalo herds were expanding east. Buffalo herds expanded into or left regions in response to conditions as well, though those conditions are still not completely understood. The Illinois became "pedestrian" buffalo hunters (hunters on foot, and not on horses).

The buffalo provided a more ample food source than the Illinois had previously known. One required adaptation was drying and preserving the meat, and the hides took a great deal of work. This was traditionally women's work, and the increased food supply required more women to do the work. A man with several wives had an advantage in acquiring wealth, so raiding for captives intensified. Women could become additional wives, and other captives could be traded with other groups.

Moreover, hunting buffalo on foot required more cooperation among hunters so villages became larger. The population of the Illinois grew to 20,000, but larger populations and more wealth attracted more attention, including attacks by the Iroquois seeking captives themselves. The combination of epidemics and attacks dropped the Illinois population to 6,000 (Morrissey 325).

In the Northeast and Great Lakes region, Indian captives were treated much like they were elsewhere. Grown men were often derided and tortured and killed. Families who had recently lost a warrior often determined a captive's fate: death or being incorporated into the family as a literal replacement. Children were often adopted into the tribe with no difference between them and children born into the group. Some captives remained slaves, and some might be made to run the gauntlet and be disfigured in the process. One Jesuit observed that the Iroquois cut off a thumb from each captive. Male captives not killed were sometimes traded as slaves, or simply given as gifts to establish friendly relations (Rushforth 782-84). As a result of all this, captives might be passed along from village to village or tribe to tribe, and thereby they could end up thousands of miles from their birthplace.

As the fur trade became the main driver of the economy in New France, captives began appearing at Montreal, and the French began to further consider slaves as a source of labor. It took the French some time to realize that in the tribal world, captives might or might not become slaves. To the tribes, captives had a ceremonial role, for example as gifts in establishing and maintaining alliances. In time, the French bought captives from their western allies and brought them east, where they could be given to friendly tribes or traded (Rushforth 798-91).

The French in the Illinois country also sometimes obtained captives and traded them to the English in the Carolinas, which happened from 1707-08, but the French authorities in Montreal and Quebec did not approve of this activity because it weakened alliances (Rushforth 799). Though the French, English and Spanish had separate colonial regions, they were linked through alliances and trade with the many Indian peoples. At the same time, their countries were typically engaged in imperial competition back in Europe and elsewhere, if not in a state of war.

After establishing an initial settlement in Quebec, the French quickly penetrated deep into the Great Lakes country seeking furs. The fur trade was the main economic activity other than subsistence farming, and this would have an impact on the systems of slavery in the region.

The French concept of slavery was vastly different from that of the tribes. To the French, a captive they bought was a chattel slave, whereas in the tribal system, captives might or might not become slaves. Captives, particularly men, were often tortured to death to satisfy the grief of a killed warrior's family, while young captives were quite often raised in the tribe as if they had been born into it. The Iroquois in particular were very prone to war and very successful at it. Their constant wars caused constant casualties, so the many captives generated during the Iroquois Wars from the 1640s to 1701 were partly to replace lost kin. Some captives were slaves doing hard work, not so different from chattel slaves, and captives to sell to the French as slaves was not as important (Demers 166-67).

At least one Iroquois was a galley slave in France. A man named Ourehouare spent two years in the galleys and was later taken back to Canada (Weaver 62-63).

One unusual feature of buying captives from tribes further to the west was their exchange for English colonists captured by the tribes in raids. The English prisoners were often ransomed. A few of these prisoners converted to Catholicism and stayed in Canada, and some, usually captured as children and adopted into a tribe, preferred to stay with their Indian families.

Among the tribes, captives were usually acquired in war, and the English settlers also enslaved Indian captives taken in war. The first war between the colonists and Indians in New England was a catastrophe for the Indians involved. The Pequot tribe was destroyed, and about 200 Pequot survivors were enslaved. Some of them were distributed among allied tribes, and a few were enslaved by New Englanders as domestic servants. The rest were sold in the West Indies (Weaver 61).

The most savage Indian war in New England, and one of the bloodiest of all the Indian wars, was King Philip's War in 1676. The fighting killed hundreds of colonists, and it destroyed Philip's people, after which hundreds of the survivors were enslaved. Most were sold in the Caribbean, but remarkably, 178 were sold in Spain and a few even reached Morocco (Weaver 61).

Indian Slavery in the Pacific Northwest

In the Pacific Northwest, a rich ecosystem based on plentiful stocks of salmon supported the development of chiefdom cultures, and these cultures featured slavery.

After Francis Drake's brief visit and hasty departure in the 16th century, the Pacific Northwest remained unvisited by whites, except perhaps for an occasional secretive Spanish expedition north from Mexico, until English Captain James Cook arrived in 1778. The Spanish, of course, had a better sense of the northwest coast of America than any other European power, but they tended to keep their discoveries to themselves, so in general, the British and French were unaware of much in the way of Spanish progress. These expeditions were, in any case, superficial, and no particular discoveries were made or documented.

Cook, on the other hand, took the same methodical approach as he had on his first two voyages, and his expedition of 1778 was recognized, for the most part, as the first modern, comprehensive mapping survey. It was certainly the first to help the Europeans actually understand the region. At the time, the parts of the coast indisputably claimed by Spain lay mainly below the 40th Parallel, and Cook was instructed not to approach the western seaboard at any point lower than that. Beyond that, he was ordered merely to proceed north along the coast to a latitude of 65 degrees, and if he found the Northwest Passage, he was to sail through it, remaining alert also for a Northeast Passage across the top of Russia. He was also to take detailed notes of possible natural resources and to take possession on behalf of the Crown any territory not claimed either by France, Spain, or Russia.

Cook

Although Cook's third expedition cost him his life and failed to locate the Northwest Passage, it did succeed in putting the Pacific Northwest on the map. Before long, fur traders and explorers were probing a coast newly mapped and documented by the Admiralty, while other notable Royal Navy expeditions, in particular that of George Vancouver, were mounted to add to the general store of knowledge. It was Vancouver who explored and mapped the Puget Sound, named for his lieutenant Peter Puget. Within two decades of Cook's death, the Pacific Northwest was a known quantity.

Vancouver

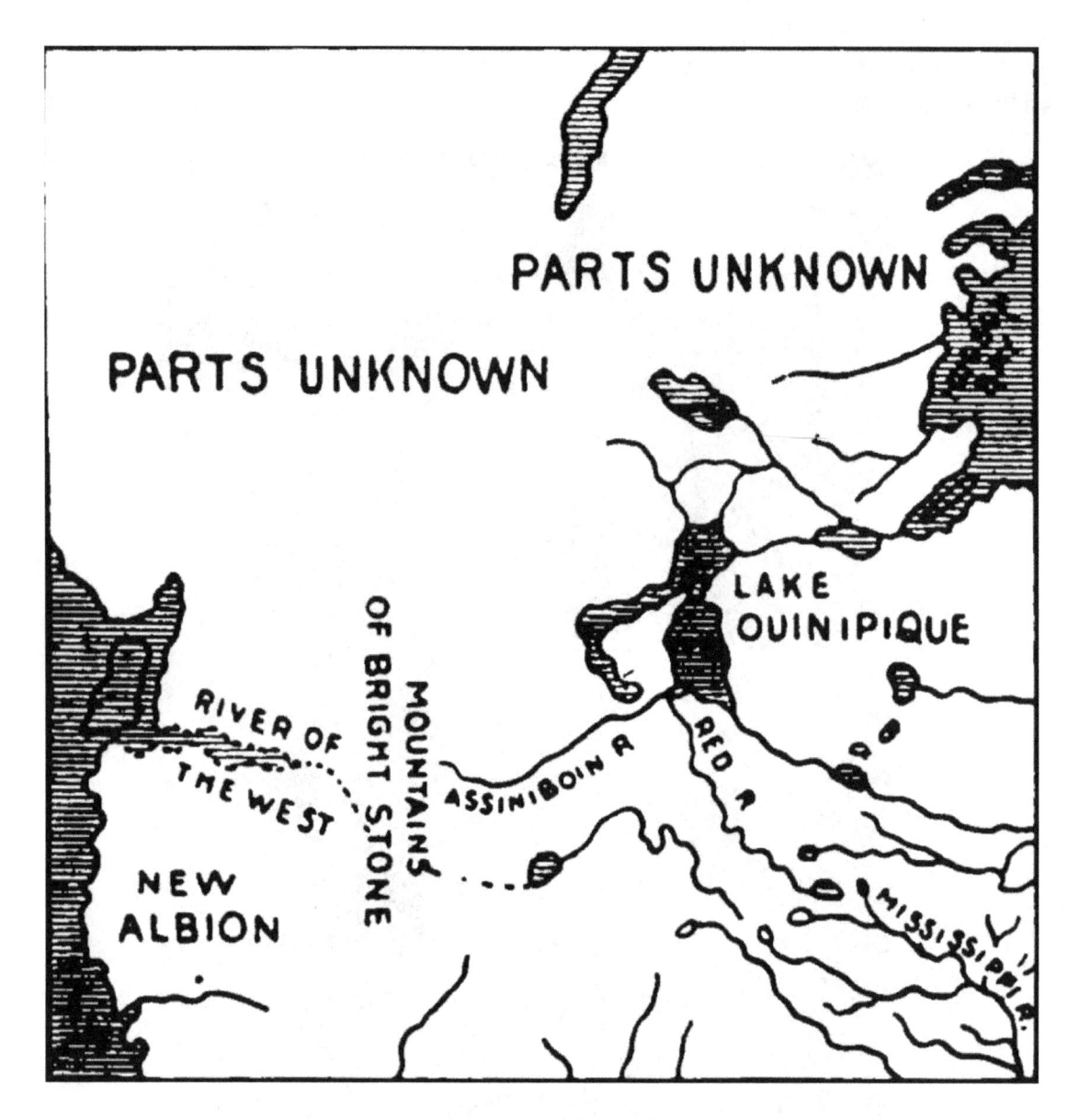

A 1778 map of the region

The catalyst of all of this, apart from the imperial ambitions of all three competing powers, was the fur trade. As Cook's men discovered in Canton, the lustrous pelt of the sea otter, the finest that nature could contrive, commanded outrageous profits, and before long traders from many nations were establishing their presence in the region. With that, Nootka Sound became the most important port of call and trading entrepôt on the coast, even as its sovereignty remained unresolved. The competition was mainly between the British and Spanish, and the first Spanish mariner to observe the port, a man named Juan Pérez, did not make a formal claim on behalf of Spain. Instead, he merely recorded a brief description of what he had seen. Cook also made no formal claim, simply because he assumed that the Spanish already had.

By the end of the 1780s, therefore, the Spanish were confident that annexation of the coast up to the point of contact with the Russians was secure. However, mainly because of the fortunes to be made in the fur trade, the British were now apt to challenge them, and the United States, anxious to develop new markets after its separation from Britain, also began to show an interest.

In the summer of 1789, Spain launched an aggressive expedition to occupy Nootka Sound, which immediately outraged British traders and prompted a diplomatic standoff between the two powers. A British merchant ship under the command of Captain James Colnett arrived in the Sound soon afterwards and was promptly seized by the Spanish, after which the British crew was sent to Mexico as prisoners. This was an extremely provocative move, and it placed the two sides near the brink of war. The crisis even engulfed the United States, which feared an imminent advance by British forces in Canada against Spanish Louisiana. The crisis was so critical that it provoked the first Cabinet-level foreign policy debate to be held in the United States under the new Constitution of 1787.

In a sign of the times, the Spanish blinked first, and the British Empire, fast becoming the strongest on the planet, emerged the winner. The Spanish agreed to claim no territory not secured by treaty or immemorial possession, which was, in effect, an almost total capitulation. This was underlined even more absolutely by a Spanish agreement to pay the British compensation for damages done to British interests in Nootka, and in due course, the Spanish began a southerly retreat that would eventually concede all of the territory north of the 42nd Parallel to the United States.

Aside from these state-sanctioned expeditions, a few outsiders visited peoples in the region in the late 18th century and estimated that about 20% of the population consisted of slaves. Chiefs had the power of life and death over them, and captives taken during the battles brought about by the region's endemic warfare were enslaved (Taylor 473).

Indeed, slavery in the Pacific Northwest can be traced back to antiquity. Archaeologists have uncovered evidence that suggests slavery existed in the region as far back as 1500 BCE, but either way, in modern times the tribal people usually had three social classes: title holders, the common people, and slaves. The slave segment of the population usually comprised those captured in war, but people could sell themselves into debt for a fixed term. Slaves might be ransomed, but it was expensive and having once been a slave was a social taint. Generally, people who became slaves remained slaves (Ames 1-3).

Slaves shared the lives of their owners, but their condition differed in several ways. Slaves were status symbols, enhancing the reputation of chiefs, and while the tasks assigned to slaves were not gendered, free commoners' tasks were highly gendered. Not surprisingly, the men who did what was considered women's work had a lower status. That work included routine but tiring chores like hauling water. A chief used slaves as soldiers and bodyguards, and they owned allegiance only to the chief. A last and basic difference of this region's slavery is that slaves could at any time be killed for any reason (Ames 3).

Some of the chiefs bought slaves. In the late 18th century, enterprising American skippers bought slaves from around the Columbia River and then sold them in the Queen Charlotte Islands for sea otter skins (Gough 160). The furs were then sold in China, where they usually fetched a good price, and Chinese luxury goods were brought for sale back in the United States. Dabbling in slaves was not the only questionable aspect of American trade with China either, because American traders eventually found opium to be a useful item in trade there.

Sea otter pelts required processing, and slaves often did this work. The sea otter population was driven nearly extinct by 1825, and after that, the fur trade switched to furs and hides from the mainland. Slaves were used in processing furs into the 1860s, and some female slaves were sold into prostitution to the Russians. In the 1790s, the small Spanish presence did not get involved in the growing trade in sea otter pelts. However, one thing they did do was buy between 150 and 200 child slaves. These Indian children were taken to Mexico to be educated as Catholics (Taylor 476).

Some of the Pacific Northwest groups practiced a unique institution called the "potlach." This was a highly ceremonial occasion of gift-giving, with a chief giving specially invited guests different kinds of gifts, including food, ceremonial objects, and slaves. The more a chief gave away, the higher their status rose, so some chiefs would give away gifts to the point of nearly impoverishing themselves. One variation of this process had competing chiefs destroy property such as clothes, carvings, and slaves, who were thus killed. The potlach continued until only one chief had anything left (Taylor 473).

A photo of a Kwakwaka'wakw potlach

A painting depicting a Klallam potlach

The ritual killing of slaves was practiced among a number of tribes in the area, but it's still unclear whether this was a rare or common activity. There is one set of numbers for one group, the Stikine, covering the years 1840-48. During that span, they ritually killed 19 slaves (Donald 81).

Some of the Pacific Northwest tribes practiced ritual cannibalism, so slaves were sometimes killed and eaten. Charges of cannibalism among American tribal peoples is hotly contested among historians and anthropologists, but the evidence of ritual cannibalism for this part of the Americas seems clear (Donald 176).

The Northwest was also the location of a kind of American slavery uncommon outside of New Mexico: white captives enslaved by Indians. Most seem to have been the survivors of shipwrecks, and while all the stories are unusual, one stands out. In 1808, Captain Nickolai Isakovich Bulagin sailed from New Archangel (Sitka), but his ship was wrecked. He and others escaped, but his wife, Anna Petrovna, did not. Bulagin tried to ransom his wife, but she preferred to remain a slave. According to the story, she ate better as a slave than as a free Russian woman in an often malnourished Sitka. Nonetheless, she died after a year or two, and like most slaves in this culture, her body was tossed in the woods (Dennis 70).

Just how many Europeans were made slaves in the Pacific Northwest is unknown, but an American captain once ransomed 12 Russians who had been made slaves by the Makah. This ransom was not done for humanitarian purposes, but apparently in anticipation of being rewarded by Russian authorities. There's also a widely told story about an American sailor who was kept naked and maltreated, with the task of gathering firewood (Donald 74-75).

The Russians did not practice slavery, but they did hold some natives in a serf-like kind of thralldom. This was particularly the case with the Aleuts, natives of the long Alaskan island chain named after them. The Russians forced the Aleuts to hunt for sea otters, often by holding the hunters' families hostage. The Aleuts and their families were treated with considerable brutality, and the traditional Aleut culture was largely destroyed because of the great profits generated from the sale of sea otter pelts in China.

The relationship between the Alaska natives and the Russians was always uneasy, but the small number of Russians and their limited means meant a relative balance of force. On one occasion, a group of Indians (probably Aleut) attacked a large group of Russian hunters and killed 200 of the 300. The survivors were then enslaved (Dennis 70).

The Royal Navy had a small base at Esquimalt on Vancouver Island whose purpose was to keep the Americans and Russians out and to support missionaries and other approved endeavors. The Royal Navy also had a slave patrol, a sort of miniature version of the slave patrols off West

Africa, but it wasn't particularly effective, given that there were reports of slavery in the Northwest as late as 1906, when news reached that young girls were still being traded as slaves (Gough 160).

Slavery in the Southwest and California

Christopher Columbus would find the New World by promoting a different route than that sought by the Portuguese, but the Portuguese explorers and traders had prepared the way for his ideas in several ways. First, the increasing confidence about long-distance sea travel, based in part on improved nautical technology and cartographical accuracy, made the notion of connecting distant regions by sea far more plausible than it had been even a hundred years earlier. For much of the Middle Ages, it was assumed that any routes connecting Europe and Asia would be land routes. Medieval cartography had always shown the possibility of sea routes, since they showed the three known continents of Europe, Asia, and Africa to be surrounded by a continuous body of water, but sea travel was regarded as far too dangerous and untested. The Portuguese explorations of the 15th century began to make this conviction look like an unfounded prejudice.

A second obstacle had been the belief, held since ancient times, that the Southern hemisphere was an uninhabitable torrid zone where life could not thrive. Now the Portuguese had traveled much farther to the south than any Europeans before them and had found the climate pleasant, the vegetation abundant, and the ground rich in mineral deposits. These discoveries found confirmation in the rediscovered work of the ancient Greek geographer Ptolemy, who had painted a relatively pleasant picture of the tropical zones of Africa. In fact, the Portuguese would find so many inhabitants of Africa that when the Pope issued his papal bulls granting the Portuguese a trade monopoly in lands they discovered in south Africa, he gave the Portuguese the "right" to make "Saracens, pagans and any other unbelievers" slaves.

The first African slaves to be transported across the Atlantic were in fact sourced from Europe itself, but very quickly trade links began to be established along the west coast of Africa for the specific purpose of sourcing slave labor. This relationship was initially pioneered by the Portuguese, but soon enough all of the major European powers had begun to adapt their international trade practices to the lucrative triangular trade in slaves, setting the pattern for the next three centuries or more of ruthless exploitation.

Towards the end of the 15th century, the British, French and to a lesser extent the Dutch entered the race to explore and chart the globe, and by extension to claim portions of it in advance of their own maritime trade. Among the great discoveries of this period were Australia in 1606, New Zealand in 1642, and Hawaii in 1778. Ultimately, however, credit for establishing the first roots of European trade along the west coast of Africa belongs to the Portuguese. The first Portuguese factory and trading post were located on the island of Arguin, located just off the coast of Mauritania, followed by a steady expansion southwards towards the coasts of Gambia and Senegal. Initial trade was limited and tended to be confined to gold, pepper and ivory, with a very limited movement of slaves supplying sugar plantations in the Mediterranean, and later Madeira. It was the Portuguese colonization of Brazil in the 16th century, however, and the establishment of commercial sugar plantations that precipitated the movement of slaves directly from West Africa to the New World, and it would be from this basis that the Transatlantic slave trade would develop.

An illustration depicting Portuguese traders in Africa

A depiction of slaves in Brazil

Perhaps inevitably, a regional rivalry developed between Spain and Portugal as the Portuguese began to establish a colony in Brazil and push its boundaries southwards. After the conquest of the Incas in the 1530s, the Portuguese threat prompted the authorization of a second expedition, commanded this time by Pedro de Mendoza with a force of some 1,500 men. The party arrived at the mouth of the Río de la Plata in 1536, and there Mendoza founded the settlement of Nuestra Señora Santa María del Buen Ayre. This was the basis of the future city of Buenos Aires, but its establishment was not without resistance from surrounding tribes. Members of the Querandí people, already familiar with Spanish methods and tactics of war from earlier encounters among the Incas, responded with violence, and in 1537, a year after its founding, Mendoza ordered the settlement abandoned. Some survivors broke ranks and sought succour among the Guaraní further upstream on the banks of the Paraná River. These early settlers assimilated reasonably easily with the Guaraní, founding the settlement of Asunción, which later became the capital city of Paraguay.

This was part of the reason the Spanish explorers and conquistadores pushed north out of Mexico into what is now the American Southwest, where they encountered some of the continent's toughest native groups.

Although the Spanish didn't formally mention the Apache until 1598, when Spanish Conquistador Don Juan de Oñate y Salazar entered the region, historians think it likely that Spanish explorer Francisco Vásquez de Coronado was referring to the Querecho Apache in 1541 when he described a group he encountered in parts of modern east New Mexico and west Texas.

Coronado wrote, "After seventeen days of travel, I came upon a 'rancheria' of the Indians who follow these cattle. These natives are called Querechos. They do not cultivate the land, but eat raw meat and drink the blood of the cattle they kill. They dress in the skins of the cattle, with which all the people in this land clothe themselves, and they have very well-constructed tents, made with tanned and greased cowhides, in which they live and which they take along as they follow the cattle. They have dogs which they load to carry their tents, poles, and belongings."

Regardless of when they encountered the Apache, the Spaniards colonized the upper Rio Grande Valley by 1598, bringing large numbers of livestock and horses to the West and Southwest. Almost immediately, the Spanish drive northward disrupted traditional Apache trade with neighboring tribes and alerted them to possible invasion. The Apache had been trading with the Pueblo and also stealing from them during raids, and once the Pueblo began to acquire horses, the Apache quickly began taking horses and adopting Spanish cavalry tactics. Crafting leather shields and chestplates, they armed themselves with Spanish-style lances (in addition to their traditional bows and arrows) and were quickly able to assume military dominance of the region. With superior numbers the key to their former battle strategies (and one reason most Apache groups never subdivided into small bands), the Apache could now take on considerably larger forces regardless of numerical disparities. Thus, by 1650, the so-called "horse frontier" was regarded by most as "Apache Territory" and was strictly avoided unless the people entering the region were prepared for confrontation.

By the early 1700s, however, the landscape changed dramatically. There was a widespread abandonment of Puebloan settlements, the migration of Coyotero and other Western Apache to points west of the Rio Grande River, the unsettling consequences of the Puebloan Revolt of 1690, and an influx of armed Comanche into Apache territories. The Comanche were superior fighters and superior raiders who frequently led successful horse-raiding missions against the Apache. All of this resulted in forcing the displacement of Apache groups. For example, the Lipan and various other Apache were forced to move south to follow their main food source (the buffalo), and there were at least seven different Native American groups now competing for resources. The displaced Apache, as well as the Suma, Jocomes, Janos, and Manso (all of whom were labeled "hostile Apache" by the Spanish) began raiding for food, and their economic structure shifted from mostly bison hunting to a raiding-hunting combination.

Apache raids on white settlements became an even bigger factor as whites pushed into the region, and the European powers also made frequent alliances to fight each other as well. The French supplied guns to indigenous groups of the Northwest, and the Spanish armed the Navajo, Ute, and Comanche. This also meant that Apache raids soon included the taking of firearms, powder and balls, and metal tools, as well as European shirts, trousers, vests, and hats. Within a century, traditional Apache garb had completely given way to white clothes. The Spanish also introduced slavery to the Apache by capturing and trading people or purchasing them as captives from other frontier groups. In time, Apache raids also took slaves along with the livestock and weaponry.

    Unsurprisingly, the Apache were hostile to the whites who came in contact with them, and the Apache were considered a big enough problem that several European nations intended to colonize the region and round up the Apache onto reservations. In 1787, the Viceroy of "New Spain", the name given to Spanish-claimed North American territory, began sending Spanish cavalry to attack Apache settlements and demand that they settle near Spanish frontier military posts, where they would receive food, liquor, and be permitted to trade. While most Apache resisted, some preferred reservation life to war, like the White Mountain Apache. Meanwhile, the Spanish governor of New Mexico, Colonel Juan Bautista de Anza, imposed a policy disallowing trade between the Apache and Navajo, while also allying with the Comanche and Ute. This served to further divide those Apache groups under Spain's watchful eye from those that were not. As ethnographer Ernest Wallace explains in *The Comanches*, "The two [Apache and Comanche] became implacable foes...and warfare prevailed between the two tribes most of the time to 1875. On the plains the Comanches were victorious, but in the hills and mountains the Apaches were able to resist successfully."

Portrait of de Anza

    By 1830, most Apache who strove to retain independence were driven to raiding (particularly of Northern Piman and Opata settlements), and they made frequent forays into Mexico, which won its independence from Spain in 1821. Generations of Apache had taken part in Mexican raids, and they thoroughly understood Mexican military tactics, knew the Mexican landscape intimately, and had come to favor Mexican women as concubines and sex captives. In fact, there were noted physical differences among various Apache groups by the early 19th century, and these differences were largely due to Apache-Mexican interaction.

As the Europeans eventually learned, the natives in the Southwest had many different cultural systems, and many involved captives. There had also been something of a trade in captives providing slaves for mines in northern Mexico, apparently predating the first Spanish settlement of New Mexico. When the Spanish began trying to settle what is now New Mexico in 1598, it was done in part to obtain captives who could be sold to the silver mines. The Spanish found a large settled population in the various Indian pueblo villages, and also a number of nomadic tribes. When Acoma Pueblo revolted, he declared that all males between 12 and 25 and all females aged 12-20 must serve 20 years of servitude (Resendez 84).

Between 1540 and 1880, thousands of Indian and Hispanic women and children were enslaved, but the real numbers will never be known. This relationship was complicated and took place in an era of change, especially once the spread of horses dramatically affected life in the region. It is thought that the massive Pueblo rebellion of 1680 resulted in sizable numbers of horses being let loose and thereby allowing the population of horses to increase exponentially. Various natives quickly exploited their potential.

By the late 17th century, the Spanish settlers in New Mexico had about 500 slaves among a population of 2,357. About half the Spanish households had a slave, but ownership of slaves was mostly concentrated in a dozen wealthy households. Slaves might also be sent south into Mexico as gifts, or to be sold.

Among the complications were the French in Louisiana and the Mississippi regions, and later the Americans. Trade involved buffalo hides that required extensive preparation, which was considered women's work. More buffalo hides meant more could be traded for items like guns, and more production required more workers, leading to a trade in women captives. French fur traders in St. Louis purchased women captives for that purpose (Brooks 48).

Over time, the trade in captives linked various peoples across a large area. In New Mexico, Governor Luis de Rosas (1637-41) experimented with slaves producing objects for sale in his Santa Fe workshop, including stockings, wool clothing, and other items for sale in Mexico. Slaves also tended orchards, gardens, and herded sheep, and since wool was important in the New Mexico economy, the slaves were needed.

Spanish punishment for Indians transgressing their rules sometimes included enslavement. In 1651, they discovered a conspiracy among the Pueblos, after which they hanged nine leaders and sold the remainder into slavery for 10 years each. In 1675, the Spanish rounded up 47 shamans, executed some, sold some into slavery, and whipped the remainder.

Tribal medicine men were usually seen by the Spanish as manifestations of Satan. One of these, a man named Po'pay, turned out to be a charismatic leader who managed to organize and lead a rebellion that killed 400 settlers and drove the Spanish out of New Mexico for a dozen years. The rebellion freed hundreds of Indians who had been enslaved (Resendez 105-06, 112).

Some of the stories of individual captives are amazing. Maria Rosa Villalpando was taken captive in 1760 at age 21 during a Comanche raid, and she was traded to the Pawnee, with whom she lived for seven years. She began cohabiting with a French fur trader, Jean Sale dit Leroie, and after she was freed, they settled in St. Louis in 1770. They had three children, but he left for France in 1792 while she remained in St. Louis. Their descendants became respected and prosperous St. Louis families before she died in 1830 (Brooks 56-57). Her story is a reminder that captives, like all slaves, are not just passive victims meekly accepting their fates.

The Comanche raided far and wide for captives, including deep into Mexico and into New Mexico, as well as raiding other tribes. They sold their first captives in New Mexico in 1710, and they continued doing so for well over a century. The Comanche often adopted younger children into the tribe who would grow up Comanche, and while captive men might be killed or sold, captive women might be sold, or kept as laborers. Sometimes captives were ransomed.

The tribe suffered high losses in their wars and raids, and the population was replenished by incorporating captive children and raising them as Comanches. Quite a large portion of Comanche ancestry consisted of captured Hispanic children growing up and becoming Comanche. They traded and sold captives to the New Mexicans, to the French in Louisiana, and even to the English. In the early 18th century, some Apache captives could be found as far away as Quebec (Resendez 127).

From 1771-1779, the region suffered droughts, made much worse by an outbreak of smallpox. As a result, several hundred New Mexico Spanish and 5,000 Pueblos died. The Comanche suffered famine and ratcheted up raiding for captives to replace their losses, as well as for horses and other goods. Between 1771 and 1776, Nueva Vizcaya in Mexico suffered 1,674 people killed in the raids, 116 haciendas abandoned, and more than 68,000 head of livestock taken (Brooks 58).

The raids worsened amidst the chaos of Mexico's efforts to become independent. Between 1816 and 1821, the Comanche took 2,000 Mexicans captive and killed as many more. In the 1830s and 1840s, they raided very deep into Mexico and took hundreds of captives (Resendez 151). A class of largely Hispanic merchants and agents emerged, most of them based in New Mexico. These Comancheros, as they came to be called, sold or traded goods to the Comanche, buying captives for resale and sometimes acting as ransom agents for a lucky few (Resendez 159).

The Navajo developed an economy based on sheep and wool (the famed Navajo blankets are one tradition emerging from this), but in the 1850s, the tribe held hundreds of captives, and these slaves were used to tend orchards, herd sheep and tend horses. A few Navajo headmen had 40-50 slaves (Resendez 166).

When American forces under the renowned Western explorer Kit Carson broke Navajo resistance in 1863 and 1864, the tribe was forced to move to a reservation called Bosque Redondo. While making their way from their home country, the Navajo became victims of slave raids by Mexicans, Anglos, and other tribes. Livestock was stolen, men were killed, and a considerable number of women and children were taken. Historians estimate that 1,000-3,000 Navajo were enslaved (Resendez 197-98).

The Utes were also formidable raiders, and like the Comanche, horses gave them plenty of mobility. In the 1830s and 1840s they raided California for horses, and the raids included some surprising participants. In 1840 the Ute Chief Walkara led 150 raiders into California in an exploit that netted 3,000 horses. One of the participants was Thomas "Peg Leg" Smith. The victims of the Utes raiding for captives tended to be Paiutes whom the Utes sold in both California and New Mexico. Paiute women could bring $150 in Santa Fe (Zappia 203).

Yet another twist on the trade in captives is that the Mormons, who began settling in Utah during the 1840s, bought Paiute children from the Utes. The Mormons sought to adopt and convert the children (Zappia 212). The number of these children remains unclear, and they may have become servants or workers in Mormon communities, but if so, these children would have been much better treated than in the brutal system in California.

There's a tendency to assume that Texas was mostly empty space until it achieved independence in 1836. That it was mostly empty space aside from the tribal lands is true, but Spanish settlement in Texas went back centuries, and Spanish and Mexican laws there were considerably less harsh on slaves than laws in the English colonies. Ultimately, Mexico abolished slavery, at least officially, and under Spanish law, Texas slaves could buy their freedom and manumission was easier. Due to interracial marriage, many slaves were light-skinned and might be branded, but Tejanos could marry without their master's consent, and those marriages could not be legally broken. A shortage of female African slaves resulted in intermarriage with Indian women. Children followed the mother's status, so the children of a free Indian woman and an African slave were free (Richmond 204-07). The situation of Afro-Tejanos deteriorated as Texas became independent and as Texas adopted the typically Southern legal regulation of slave status.

There is a generally unknown slavery in the history of California, and it involved a particularly savage form of slavery that victimized almost as many as the Carolina slave trade a century and a half earlier. California was acquired in the aftermath of the war with Mexico and was lightly populated, with a few thousand Californios (Mexican Californians) and a few thousand others, from a few mountain men left over from fur-trading days to newcomers like the Swiss immigrant

John Sutter. There were also about 150,000 Indians.

Sutter was an immigrant with ambitions. He was a slave raider on a considerable scale to obtain Indian labor for his ambitious schemes (Resendez 174). He set up various businesses and farms, and he arranged for a mill to be constructed. In the process of building it in 1848, traces of gold were found. More gold was found, and a stampede occurred. The California Gold Rush brought tens of thousands of prospectors to the territory by the end of 1848, and the floodgates opened in 1849. By 1852, California had become a state with more than 200,000 people.

Some of the California Indians had been forcibly resettled in the missions founded by the Spanish in the late 1700s. They were Christianized and became participants in a program designed to turn them into docile peasants. The missions were on their own during the chaos resulting from the troubles in Mexico that eventually resulted in Mexican independence. Mexico dissolved the missions, and they were taken over by Californio families. The richer families prospered in the hide and tallow trade that developed, and the mission Indians largely became laborers on ranches. It was not exactly slavery, but it was often a kind of bondage, most often debt peonage. In 1846, perhaps 20,000 Indians were in various forms of bondage, including most of the workforce that John Sutter used in building his small empire (Madley 625).

Sutter

The Gold Rush overwhelmed the ranchos and everything else in California, and prospectors all but inherited the mission system of exploiting the Indians. The specific California situation not only had its roots in the mission practices of forced labor, but also Californian customs. While the initial Gold Rush heavily emphasized mining for gold, the economy developed rapidly, including ranches, many small towns, and some farming, so Indians were a convenient source of labor. A peculiar feature of California was an intense contempt for Indians who existed primarily in the hunter-gatherer societies and struck most of the immigrants to California as the lowest level of humanity. In California, the Indian peoples existed largely in the band stage, less organized and less impressive than the formidable Eastern and Plains tribes.

The prospectors who rushed to California were quite diverse, including Chileans, Mexicans, Chinese, Australians, and Americans from all over the country. By far the largest of the gold-seeking migrants, Americans quickly took control and set up a state government. It immediately limited voting to white males, and the legislature also passed a benign-sounding legislation called "An Act for the Government and Protection of Indians." The Act was really a means of controlling Indian labor. Slavery based on African Americans was disliked in California, and when California became a state, it entered the Union as a free state. However, it developed a different kind of slavery that was as bad as anything in the South, and arguably even more violent. California slavery in effect dovetailed with genocide. It was illegal to sell Indians arms or ammunition, and an Indian could not give testimony against any white person in a criminal trial.

The Act allowed for Indian children to be held and worked without pay until age 15 for women and 18 for men. In theory, it was to help orphan children, but it resulted in hundreds of children simply being taken from their parents, and those children often became orphans because raiders killed their parents.

The legislation also included a vagrancy law. Indians who were found loitering around, begging, or leading an "immoral or profligate" life could be arrested by any white citizen. The arrested Indians were to be taken to a magistrate and jailed, and the law required that the Indian could then be leased to the highest bidder. The Indians of course were fined, could not pay the fine, and had to work to pay off the fine. Bidders could hold and work these manufactured convicts for four months without pay (Madley 643).

The legislation was soon revised to allow long unpaid indentures for Indian children. Children could be indentured until age 21, and 25 or 30 depending on conditions. A 10-year indenture could be imposed on Indians over age 20 (Madley 650).

These conditions resembled the vagrancy laws in the South after the Civil War that forced tens of thousands of black men into the convict leasing system, and that system lasted into the 1920s. How many Indians were slaves in California is unknown, but in total it must have been in the tens of thousands. The California population reached 553,000 in 1870, so the shortage of labor gradually faded, and this unusual system of slavery was mostly gone by the 1860s. It was no coincidence that this system's demise coincided with the drastic drop in native populations, which went from 150,000 to less than 15,000 by 1870.

Indian Owners of African Slaves

Depending on the era, reaching native land was a tempting option for escaped slaves, especially in Florida. As early as 1687, a group of slaves escaping from Georgia arrived in Florida in a stolen canoe, consisting of eight men, two women, and a baby. They reached St. Augustine and requested Catholic baptism.

St. Augustine was a pitifully defended place, largely relying on a company of mixed race and free black men, augmented by Indians and a scattering of Spanish, but they fought well enough to repel an attack by French pirates in 1686 (Landers 497, 489). The pirates may have been doing some speculative slave raiding themselves, because captured Indians, African slaves, and freedmen were all readily sold in the Caribbean.

The main Indian slaveholders of African slaves were the "Five Civilized Tribes" (Choctaw, Chickasaw, Creek, Cherokee, and Seminole), a name given to the five groups by white people who were impressed with the "progress" the tribes made to what was considered civilization. These peoples lived in the Southeast, and as the white population sharply increased, many members of these tribes settled and took to farming as a way to cope with change. Some of them were prosperous and able to buy black slaves and establish plantations. Between the end of the wars with settlers and the period of Indian Removal in the 1830s, several of the tribes set up tribal governments based on the U.S. Constitution (Krauthamer 15). A Cherokee man, Sequoyah, developed a script for the Cherokee language, and the Cherokee nation even developed newspapers.

Adapting to African slavery was a gradual process. The Creeks acquired their first African slaves in the 1760s, and by then they had a century of experience dealing with white owners of black slaves. Early on, the Creeks had been both slave raiders and victims of the slave trade, and the first treaty between the Georgia Trustees (the authorities in Georgia at the time) and the Creeks called for the return of escaped slaves. Return of an escaped slave was rewarded with two guns or four blankets, or they got one blanket for the escaped slave's head (Braund 611). Some of the tasks assigned to slaves by white slaveholders, such as gardening and gathering firewood, were what the Creeks thought of as women's work, which contributed to Indian opinions of African slaves.

During the Revolution, the Creeks were divided as to which side to support. Some raided Georgia and the Carolinas, where they captured a sizable number of slaves to trade or sell to white buyers. Those buyers then typically sold them in Florida and in Louisiana (Braund 618-19).

Black slaves owned by the Creeks were slaves, but there was one important difference: some escaped slaves were admitted to the tribe, and the children of an escaped slave and a Creek woman were accepted into the tribe. The child of a Creek mother was always a Creek, and while ancient matrilineal tradition gave way to the patriarchal mainstream American views in time, tribal membership remained automatic for the children of a Creek woman. Slaves were slaves and were seen as inferior, but the elaborate social structure of racial supremacy seems to have been far milder among the Creeks. Also, slaves and their Creek owners lived in close proximity, not in separate quarters.

There is some evidence that when a prominent Creek died, his slaves, horses, and cattle were put to death, but the practice was stopped by the Creek leader Alexander McGillivray (Braund 626).

The Seminoles in Florida were something of an exception to altering their lifestyle, mostly continuing traditional ways in the Florida wilderness and fighting three especially stubborn wars with the United States. The Seminoles did practice a more mild form of slavery, and the stout resistance of black Seminoles was one reason the wars were so deadly for American troops.

The Southeastern Indians absorbed to an extent the slaveholder ideology of African inferiority, and the ownership and employment of African slaves evolved gradually. In 1809, the 12,000 Cherokee owned 583 black slaves, but by 1825, the 14,000 Cherokee owned 1,277 slaves. In 1836, 15,000 Cherokee owned 1,592 slaves (McLoughlin 379-80). The gradual increase in slave numbers can be taken as a rough measure of the tribes' assimilation, which ultimately didn't save them from being forced out of their homelands to make way for white settlers. An additional factor was the 1829-30 gold rush in north Georgia, during which thousands of prospectors and squatters overran Cherokee territory.

During the removal process, the tribes were allowed to keep their slaves, which is somewhat surprising because slaves were quite valuable property. A great deal of Indian property was simply seized by whites, such as farms, livestock, orchards, crops in the field, agricultural equipment, horses, barns, and wagons.

The most famous part of the sad chapter of Indian removal was the Trail of Tears, which devastated the Cherokee, but the removal also pushed 15,000 Choctaws and 3,000 Chickasaws to Indian Territory. They were merged into a single "nation" from the time of the removal to 1855. By the time they were being removed, these tribes had largely absorbed mainstream concepts of social organization and property. Traditionally, both tribes were matrilineal, so a boy's maternal uncles would be the main male influence in his life. They also allowed sororal polygamy in which several sisters might marry the same man.

Traditionally, captives might be killed, absorbed into the tribe as full members, or retained as slaves, but the tribes changed from traditional life ways to accepting the predominating

American concepts in the early 1800s. They became more paternal-oriented, and slaves became more fully chattel property than they had been (Krauthamer 49).

Indian slaveholders were not kinder to slaves just because they also suffered discrimination at the hands of the white majority. In Indian Territory, there are accounts of slaves rebelling and killing their owners, and of the same kind of gruesome suppression of slave resistance that characterized the South (Krauthamer 75-79). Indeed, once they were settled in the Indian Territory, the natives' laws showed the influence of Southern models. Their legal codes enshrined racial differences more fully than had existed in their original homelands. The Choctaws did not permit a free black person, or anyone descended from such a person, to become a citizen of the Choctaw Nation, while the Chickasaws barred black people or "anyone part Negro" from citizenship, suffrage or holding office" (Krauthamer 37). In 1841, the Cherokees banned slaves from carrying weapons, and in 1848 anyone caught teaching slaves to read or write was to be expelled from the Cherokee Nation (McLaughlin 381).

There were a few free black people in the Choctaw and Chickasaw during the Civil War. Despite their alliance with the Confederacy, raiders sometimes kidnapped free black people and sold them into slavery (Krauthamer 64-65).

Indian Territory was a quite unusual territory. It was bought by the federal government via the Louisiana Purchase in 1803, but it remained sparsely settled. It was not a state and not a territory in the usual sense, as territories usually were seen as states in the making, joining the Union when the population became large enough and the area was developed enough.

Instead, Indian Territory was broken into a number of regions, assigned to particular tribes that then governed it. These governed areas were usually referred to as Indian "nations," and they had in effect a kind of home rule that was a de facto independence. The relationships between individual tribes and the federal government were regulated by formal treaties, and the agreements by which tribes ceded their lands east of the Mississippi often gave the tribes goods or specified amounts of money per year, as well as land in Indian Territory. Of course, these treaties were almost always lopsided and then violated, and tribes already living in the region were not consulted, so there was some fighting between the resettled peoples and the ones for whom Oklahoma had been their traditional hunting grounds.

Indian Territory was not a state, but it was a slave territory. At the time of the outbreak of the Civil War, about 8,000 of the 100,000 inhabitants of the Territory were slaves. Indian slaveholders were close to Bloody Kansas, which pitted abolitionists and pro-slavery groups in violent conflicts against each other during the 1850s. Like Southerners, the Indian slaveholders were worried about Abraham Lincoln's election in 1860.

There were several reasons why joining the Confederacy appealed to a substantial number of Indians in the Territory. They were not happy with the slowness of the federal government in supplying annuity payments guaranteed by various treaties, or by the government's tendency to neglect treaty obligations. They were also aware that one of Lincoln's advisers, Secretary of State William H. Seward, had recommended appropriating land in the Territory and opening it to settlers. Trade ties in the Territory were largely Southern, and most of the federal Indian agents had been Southerners. Some families were blood-related to prominent Southern families, and some prominent Indians owned plantations which used slaves to produce commodities for sale, in the common Southern manner.

Indian slaveowners had the same concerns about Lincoln's election as white slaveowners did. They were uneasy about abolitionist sentiment and concerned about the future of slave ownership. At the same time, Indian Territory was not a state, but a collection of self-governing tribes, so it could not secede from the Union in the same manner as the Confederate states. Abrogating treaties with the federal government and signing with the Confederacy amounted to secession (Gibson 387-88).

At the start of the war, the Union troops in Indian Territory were under the command of Colonel William Emory. Troops had protected the Territory from raids from Plains Indians, and policed intruders, but in May of 1861, Colonel Emory ordered three forts to be abandoned and pulled all the troops out of the Territory. This removed all military protection and effectively removed the federal government's presence.

Emory

The key early Confederate figure was Albert Pike, who was born in New England, lived in Arkansas for years, and practiced law. He seems to have been quite well educated, credited with knowing French, Greek, Latin, Spanish, several Indian languages, and Sanskrit, which was exceedingly rare in Arkansas (Hauptman 26). The fact that he knew Indian languages was unusual and may indicate that Pike liked and respected Indians.

Pike

Pike was named the Confederate Commissioner of Indian Affairs, but there was no Confederate bureaucracy charged with relations with the tribes, as there was in Washington. Thus, even as Pike was made a Commissioner, his role was not particularly well defined, so his initiative largely created Confederate policy when it came to dealing with the Indians. It was not clear whether the tribes were going to participate in the Civil War, but Indian Territory had strategic importance as a buffer for Texas and Arkansas, and as a route to Kansas and Missouri. It was also a potential gateway for the expansion of the Confederacy to the west.

Meeting with Chickasaw and Choctaw leaders, Pike negotiated a treaty covering 64 specific terms involving Chickasaw and Choctaw national sovereignty, possibilities of Confederate citizenship, and an entitled delegate in the House of Representatives of the Confederate States of America. Since the Chickasaw had slaves, resented the federal government for forcing them off their lands, and were upset that the government failed to protect them from the Plains Indian tribes, the Chickasaw Nation became the first of the Five Civilized Tribes to become allies of the Confederates. Passing a tribal resolution formally allying with the Confederacy, Captain Julius Caesar Folsom, a Chickasaw by blood, wrote, "Up to this time, our protection was in the United States troops stationed at Fort Washita, under the command of Colonel Emory. But he, as soon as the Confederate troops had entered our country, at once abandoned us and the Fort; and, to make his flight more expeditious and his escape more sure, employed Black Beaver, a Shawnee Indian, under a promise to him of five thousand dollars, to pilot him and his troops out of the Indian country safely without a collision with the Texas Confederates; which Black Beaver accomplished. By this act the United States abandoned the Choctaws and Chickasaws . . . Then, there being no other alternative by which to save their country and property, they, as the less of the two evils that confronted them, went with the Southern Confederacy." Folsom would subsequently join Green Thompson's Chickasaw-Choctaw command and fight during the Civil War throughout Indian Territory, Missouri, and Texas.

Meanwhile, throughout the summer and fall of 1861, Pike signed treaties with several of the tribes, including the Quapaw, Seneca, Shawnee and Osage. The treaties that Pike signed with the Indian nations were moderate. All treaties with the federal government were abrogated, and the Confederacy would assume the annuity payments previously paid by Washington. Indian rights to their land were guaranteed, the right to own slaves was guaranteed, and the Confederacy would protect the tribes from invaders.

The treaties stipulated that the Confederacy was to establish a postal system, and the treaties specified that the Confederacy had the right to build military posts and the right of way for telegraph and railroad development. Indian troops would be paid by the Confederate government, and most importantly, Indian troops would not be required to serve outside of Indian Territory (Warde 54).

The Cherokee didn't sign any agreement at first, because Principal Chief John Ross proclaimed Cherokee neutrality. Cherokee neutrality officially continued until Ross was captured and interned by Union troops, after which Stand Watie signed a treaty with the Confederates. In 1863, Union Colonel William Phillips was placed in charge of organizing the Union Cherokee. He convened the "Cowskin Prairie Council," at which the Union Cherokee repudiated the treaty with the Confederates and elected Thomas Pegg as acting Principal Chief (Ross was under house arrest in Philadelphia). At the same time, the Confederates recognized Watie as Principal Chief of the Cherokee Nation.

Indian slaveholding of African slaves did not end in the same way as it did in the South. A council was called for Ft. Smith in September of 1865, but it was aborted, and in early 1866 a different council met in Washington. These Reconstruction-era treaties shuffled around Indian lands, and the tribes were forced to allow railroad development and required that slavery be ended. It also required that the freed slaves be given land. Unlike in the South, freedom in Indian Territory actually did bring an approximation of 40 acres and a mule (Gibson 486).

Black Slaveowners

There are known to have been several thousand free blacks who owned slaves, and inevitably the nature of this slavery is hotly debated. The numbers are based on estimates from census data. One view of African Americans owning other African Americans is what has been called "benevolent slavery," which begs the question of how any kind of slavery could be considered benevolent. Not surprisingly, the explanation is a bit complicated.

Most slave states had restrictions on the manumissions of slaves by their owners and the ability for slaves to buy their freedom. There was a deep suspicion of free black people; Virginia, for example, demanded than manumitted slaves leave Virginia in one year or be re-enslaved. A grandfather clause permitted already free black people to remain, and a free African American could purchase spouses, children, and relatives, but technically freeing them would require them to leave the state. As a result, remaining in a technical state of being owned was actually a means of keeping a family together, which brought about the concept of "benevolent slavery." (Lightner and Ragan 536-37).

The oldest known case of an African American owning slaves is in Virginia in the mid-1600s, when a black man named Anthony Johnson on Virginia's Eastern Shore owned slaves, but limitations on black slaveholders were rapidly imposed. This was during the brief era when the legal confusion over indenture and chattel slavery was still being worked out. After 1728, Virginia made it much more difficult to free a slave (Schwarz 321).

The extent of slaveholding by African Americans is unknown. In 1830, there were 3,776 black slaveholders in all with 12,907 slaves (Pressley 85).

The core of the debate about African American slaveholding is whether they were benevolent or exploitative. The evidence suggests both existed.

African American slave ownership peaked in 1830, and in that year about 1,000 of 55,000 free blacks in Virginia owned slaves. After 1830, Virginia law was changed so that black slaveholders could acquire no more slaves except spouses, children, and slaves gained via birth (Schwarz 319-21).

Not surprisingly, some of the stories involving black slaveowners are unique. John Carruthers Stanly was born a slave in North Carolina in 1774. He was trained as a barber, and he was presumably a good one because he was freed at age 21. He prospered enough to buy his wife and five children in 1805, and later he bought two slaves and trained them as barbers. This was plainly more of an exploitative form of slavery because Stanley took their earnings. Stanly became wealthy, and at the height of his fortunes in 1830 he owned three plantations totaling 2,600 acres. With 163 slaves working for him, Stanly was the largest black slaveholder in the South, but he eventually lost most of them by co-signing a note for his white half-brother. By 1840, he owned seven slaves (Lightner and Ragan 538-40).

Another story is that of William Ellison, born a slave in South Carolina in 1790. Somehow, he had the opportunity to learn how to build and repair cotton gins. At age 26 he bought his own freedom, and then he bought his wife and daughter. He also bought four slaves and trained them to work in his shop. He became a planter, and eventually he had 900 acres being worked by 63 slaves, none of which he ever freed. Ellison died in 1861, but his family remained prosperous. There's a sad irony in the fact that the family's wealth was invested in slaves and Confederate bonds (Lightner and Ragan 540-41).

There were other black slaveholders in Virginia as the Civil War approached. A man named Jacob Simpson had 11 slaves working 500 acres of land in 1860. Also in 1860, Frank Miles had 19 slaves working 1,100 acres, and Priscilla Ivey had slaves working 1,304 acres from 1821-1856 (Schwarz 328).

In general, the largest operations owned by African American slaveholders were in Louisiana. In 1860, Auguste Donato of St. Landry Parish had 70 slaves working 500 acres of land, and during that same year, Ciprien Ricard and her son Pierre owned 168 slaves in Iberville Parish. In 1859, they had produced 515 hogsheads of sugar (a hogshead was a large barrel, and a hogshead of sugar would be 800-1,500 pounds).

Black slaveholders were scattered widely. In 1830, there were 11 such slaveholders personally residing in New York City (Koger).

Restrictions on freed slaves were heavy, and in 1829 in some states it was illegal to teach freed slaves to read or write. Poll taxes, fines, expensive licenses for some trades, and requirements to register annually were among the restrictions imposed (Lightner and Ragan 537).

Benevolent slavery was a way to avoid some of these restrictions, but as some of the examples above indicate, some black slaveowners were just as determined to wring a profit out of their slaves as white owners were. The extent of the exploitative kind of slavery and the benevolent kind of slavery can only be estimated, but some research indicates that the exploitative form of slavery on the part of African American slaveholders was more common in the lower South (Lightner and Ragan 553).

The End of Slavery

American schoolchildren are taught that slavery formally ended in the wake of the Civil War, particularly with the passage of the 13th Amendment, but slavery certainly didn't end in 1865.

The courts largely interpreted the 13th Amendment as applying to African American slaves, and a clause in the 13th Amendment also banned "involuntary servitude" except as punishment for convicted criminals.

The "involuntary servitude" language did give authorities the possibility of going after debt peonage and even using Indian slaves. In 1865, there were still 1,500-3,000 slaves in New Mexico, and some of them were held in a perpetual state of indebtedness, with pay so low that it didn't cover the costs for room and board, which was then added to the debt. In 1867, Congress passed legislation that came to be called "The Peonage Act of 1867," and it threatened $5,000 fines and five years in prison, but it is not clear if anyone was ever convicted (Resendez 209). In fact, versions of the peonage system in the state lasted into the 1960s.

In 1868, General William Tecumseh Sherman visited Bosque Redondo. He was not particularly sympathetic to Indians in general, but what he found there he found appalling. Sherman was a member of a commission authorized by Congress to use any reasonable means to reclaim Indians from bondage, and several hundred Navajos and others were freed (Resendez 210-11).

California's system of indenturing Indian children died a slow death. As late as the 1870s, there were somewhere around 1,500 (Resendez 207).

Then there is the grim history of the convict leasing system in some of the Southern states. The system was designed to produce cheap and controllable labor, so states passed vagrancy laws and local authorities would accost people who looked homeless while lounging around, sometimes strangers. In Florida, if they had less than $5 in their pocket, they could be arrested as vagrants. The vagrants were arrested and fined, and since they could not pay the fines and accompanying court costs, they were sentenced to jail. They were then rented out to companies.

Vagrants were only part of the system, and since they were convicts, they had no rights to complain and no protections as workers.

Leasing out convicts was common in the "Naval Stores" industry (the production of pitch and turpentine from pine forests), but it also produced workers for mines and iron foundries. Most of the leased convicts were black, as were most men arrested for vagrancy. Discipline was maintained pretty much the same way slavery was: the liberal use of beatings and the whip.

This new form of slavery existed in most Southern states and lasted well into the 1900s. An estimated 100,000 people were caught up in the system over the years it existed.

While these forms of slavery have all been formally abolished, slavery still exists in the 21st century, mostly in the form of human trafficking. The Global Slavery Index says there are 403,000 people living in conditions of slavery in the United States as of 2019.

Online Resources

<u>Other books about colonial American history by Charles River Editors</u>

<u>Other books about slavery on Amazon</u>

Further Reading

Ablavsky, George. "Making Indians 'White': The Judicial Abolition of Native Slavery in Virginia and Its Racial Legacy." *University of Pennsylvania Law Review* 159 (5), April 2011. 1457-1531.

Ames, Kenneth M. "Slaves, Chiefs and Labor in the Northern Northwest Coast." *World Archaeology* 33 (1), June 2001. 1-17.

Braund, Kathryn E. Holland. "The Creek Indians, Blacks, and Slavery." *Journal of Southern History* 57 (4). 601-636.

Brooks, James F. *Captives and Cousins: Slavery, Kinship and Community in the Southwest Borderlands*. Chapel Hill, University of North Carolina Press, 2002.

Brown. Philip. "Early Indian Trade in the Development of South Carolina: Politics, Economics, and Social Mobility During the Proprietary Period 1660-1719." *The South Carolina Historical Magazine* 76 (3), July 1975. 118-128.

Demers, E.A.S. "Native American Slavery and Territoriality in the Colonial Upper Great Lakes Region." *Michigan Historical Review*, 28 (2) Fall 2002. 163-172.

Dennis, Elsie Frances. "Indian Slavery in the Pacific Northwest." *Oregon Historical Quarterly* 31 (1) March 1930. 69-81.

Donald, Leland. *Aboriginal Slavery on the Northwest Coast of North America*. Berkeley: University of California Press, 1997.

Gallay, Alan. *The Indian Slave Trade: The Rise of the English Empire in the American South 1670-1717*. New Haven: Yale University Press, 2002.

Gibson, Arrell Morgan. "Native Americans and the Civil War." *American Indian Quarterly* 9 (4), Fall 1985. 385-410.

Gough, Barry. "Send a Gunboat! Checking Slavery and Controlling Liquor Traffic Among Coast Indians of British Columbia in the 1860s." *The Pacific Northwest Quarterly* 69 (4), October 1978. 159-168.

Hardy, James D. "The Transportation of Convicts to Colonial Louisiana." *Louisiana History* 7

(3), Summer 1996. 207-220.

Koger, Larry. "Black Slave Owners." The Abbeville Institute Blog. abbevilleinstitute.org/blog/ black-slaveowners/ January 7, 2016. Accessed September 30, 2019.

Krauthamer, Barbara. *Black Slaves, Indian Masters*. Chapel Hill, University of North Carolina Press, 2013.

Landers, Jane. "The Geopolitics of Seventeenth Century Florida." *The Florida Historical Quarterly* 92 (3), Winter 2014. 480-490.

Lightner, David L., and Ragan, Alexander. "Were African American Slaveholders Benevolent or Exploitative? A Quantitative Approach." *The Journal of Southern History* 71 (3), August 2005. 535-558.

Madley, Benjamin. "Unholy Traffic in Human Blood and Souls: Systems of California Indian Servitude Under U.S. Rule." *Pacific Historical Review* 83 (4), November 2014. 626-667.

McLaughlin, William. "Red Indians, Black Slavery and White Racism: America's Slaveholding Indians." *American Quarterly*, 26 (4), October 1974. 367-385.

Morgan, Kenneth. "English and American Attitudes Towards Convict Transportation 1718-1775." *History* 72 (236), October 1987. 416-431.

_____. "Convict Runaways in Maryland. 1745-1775." *Journal of American Studies* 23 (2) August 1989. 253-268.

Morrissey Robert M. "Bison Algonquians: Cycles of Violence and Exploitation in the Mississippi Valley Borderlands." *Early American Studies* 13 (2), Spring, 2015. 309-340.

Pressley, Thomas J. "The 'Known World' of Free Black Slaveholders: A Research Note on the Scholarship of Carter G. Woodson." *Journal of African American History* 91 (1), Winter 2006. 81-87.

Resendez, Andres. *The Other Slavery: The Uncovered Story of Indian Enslavement in America*. New York: Houghton Mifflin, 2015.

Richmond, Douglas. "African's Initial Encounter with Texas: The Significance of Afro-Tejanos in Colonial Texas 1528-1821. *Bulletin of African American Research*, 26 (2) April 2007. 200-221.

Rushforth, Brett. "A Little Flesh We Offer You: The Origin of Indian Slavery in New France." *The William and Mary Quarterly* 60 (4), October 2003. 777-808.

Schwarz, Philip J. "Emancipators, Protection and Anomalies: Free Black Slaveowners in Virginia." *The Virginia Magazine of History and Biography*, 95 (3), July 1987. 317-338.

Taylor, Alan. *American Colonies: The Settling of America*. New York: Penguin, 2001.

Weaver, Jace. *The Red Atlantic: American Indians and the Making of the Modern World 1000-1927*. Chapel Hill: University of North Carolina Press, 2014.

Webre, Stephen. "The Problem of Indian Slavery in Spanish Louisiana, 1769-1803." *Louisiana History* 25 (2), Spring 1984. 117-135.

Worth, John E. "Razing Florida: The Indian Slave Trade and the Destruction of Spanish Florida, 659-1715." In Ethridge, Robbie and Shuck-Hall, Sheri, *Mapping the Mississippian Shatter Zone: The Colonial Indian Slave Trade and Regional Instability in the American South*. Lincoln: University of Nebraska Press, 2009.

Zappia, Natalie A. Indigenous Borderlands: Livestock, Captivity and Power in the Far West." *Pacific Historical Review* 81 (2), May 2012. 193-220.

Free Books by Charles River Editors

We have brand new titles available for free most days of the week. To see which of our titles are currently free, click on this link.

Discounted Books by Charles River Editors

We have titles at a discount price of just 99 cents everyday. To see which of our titles are currently 99 cents, click on this link.

CPSIA information can be obtained
at www.ICGtesting.com
Printed in the USA
LVHW060409120722
723285LV00012B/235